W9-AJP-841

Bre

Sea Turtles
and Other Shelled Reptiles

Concept and Product Development: Editorial Options, Inc.
Series Designer: Karen Donica
Book Author: Patricia Brennan

For information on other World Book
products, visit us at our Web site at
http://www.worldbook.com

For information on sales to schools and libraries
in the United States, call 1-800-975-3250.

For information on sales to schools and libraries
in Canada, call 1-800-837-5365.

World Book, Inc.
233 N. Michigan Avenue
Chicago, IL 60601

Library of Congress Cataloging-in-Publication Data

Brennan, Patricia.
     Sea turtles and other shelled reptiles.
       p. cm. -- (World Book's animals of the world)
     Summary: Questions and answers provide information about a variety of turtles,
     including sea turtles, Galapagos tortoises, and alligator snapping turtles.
     ISBN 0-7166-1231-3 -- ISBN 0-7166-1223-2 (set)
     1. Sea turtles--Juvenile literature. 2. Turtles--Juvenile literature. [1. Sea
turtles--Miscellanea. 2. Turtles--Miscellanea. 3. Questions and answers.] I. Title. II.
Series.
     QL666.C536 B74 2002
     597.92'8--dc21   2001046715

Printed in Malaysia

1 2 3 4 5 6 7 8 9 06 05 04 03 02

Picture Acknowledgments: Front & Back Cover: © Andrew G. Wood, Photo Researchers; © Mitsuaki Iwago, Minden Pictures; © Tom & Pat Leeson, Photo Researchers; © Steve Maslowski, Photo Researchers; © Gary Meszaros, Bruce Coleman Inc.

© Mark Bacon, Bruce Coleman Inc. 31; © Fred Bavendam, Minden Pictures 13; © Tom Brakefield, Bruce Coleman Inc. 9; © Steve Cooper, Photo Researchers 43; © Tui DeRoy, Bruce Coleman Inc. 35. 37; © Jim W. Grace, Photo Researchers 39; © David Hughes, Bruce Coleman Inc. 21; © Mitsuaki Iwago, Minden Pictures 25; © Tom & Pat Leeson, Photo Researchers 4, 33; © Zig Leszczynski, Animals Animals 51, 55; © Renee Lynn, Photo Researchers 9; © Steve Maslowski, Photo Researchers 47; © Fred McConnaughey, Photo Researchers 61; © Tom McHugh, Photo Researchers 29, 57; © Gary Meszaros, Bruce Coleman Inc. 45; © Mark Newman, Bruce Coleman Inc. 27; © Barry E. Parker, Bruce Coleman Inc. 23; © Laura Riley, Bruce Coleman Inc. 9; © Leonard Lee Rue III, Photo Researchers 59; © John Serrao, Photo Researchers 53; © Dan Suzio, Photo Researchers 41; © Norman Owen Tomalin, Bruce Coleman Inc. 9; © Bruce Watkins, Animals Animals 5, 19; © James Watt, Animals Animals 5, 7; © Doug Wechsler, Animals Animals 49; © Andrew G. Wood, Photo Researchers 3, 15, 17.

Illustrations: WORLD BOOK illustration by Michael DiGiorgio 11, WORLD BOOK illustration by Kersti Mack 62.

World Book's Animals of the World

Sea Turtles
and Other Shelled Reptiles

What kind of race can I win?

World Book, Inc.
A Scott Fetzer Company
Chicago

Contents

Can you find anything catlike about me?

What sends me packing for warmer waters?

Do you want to race with me?

What Are Shelled Reptiles?

Reptiles are a large group of animals. Reptiles have dry, scaly skin. They use lungs to breathe. But only one group of reptiles—the turtles—has shells.

There are many species, or kinds, of turtles. Terrapins are turtles. So are desert tortoises and snapping turtles. And, as you might guess from the name, sea turtles are turtles, too.

A turtle's shell is actually part of its skeleton. All reptiles have skeletons *inside* their bodies—just as you do. But turtles also wear part of their skeleton on the *outside*.

Like all reptiles, turtles are cold-blooded. That means that the temperature of a turtle's body changes with the temperature of its surroundings. If it's warm outside, the turtle is warm. And if it's cold outside, the turtle is cold. If it gets too cold, a turtle can't be active or may not even be able to move.

Sea turtle

Where in the World Do Turtles Live?

Since turtles are cold-blooded, they can't live in places that are cold all year long. But turtles live almost everywhere else. They live in hot, sandy deserts. They live in lush, green forests and grasslands. Some turtles live high in the mountains. Others live in wet, lowland marshes and swamps.

Besides living on land, turtles also live in water. Many kinds of turtles live in fresh water, such as in lakes, ponds, or rivers. Sea turtles live in salty oceans.

Altogether, there are seven species of turtles that live in the sea. Most kinds live in more than one ocean. Green turtles, for example, live in the Atlantic, Pacific, and Indian oceans. Other kinds of sea turtles, such as Kemp's ridleys, have a much smaller area they call home. This sea turtle is found only in the Gulf of Mexico and some parts of the Atlantic Ocean.

Desert

Forest

Swamp

Sea

What Is a Sea Turtle's Shell Like?

Most sea turtles have hard shells that are like suits of armor. A hard shell is made up of several plates. These plates fit together like pieces in a jigsaw puzzle. They make the shell firm and tough. Even a shark's razor-sharp teeth can't bite through it.

The curved shell on a sea turtle's back is called the *carapace (KAR uh pays)*. A sea turtle doesn't just have a shell on its back, though. It also has a shell called the *plastron (PLAS truhn)* that covers its belly. On most turtles, hard scales cover the parts of the body that are not protected by the shell.

The shell has openings for the turtle's head, tail, and legs. Sea turtles have legs shaped like long paddles, with flippers instead of feet.

Diagram of a Turtle

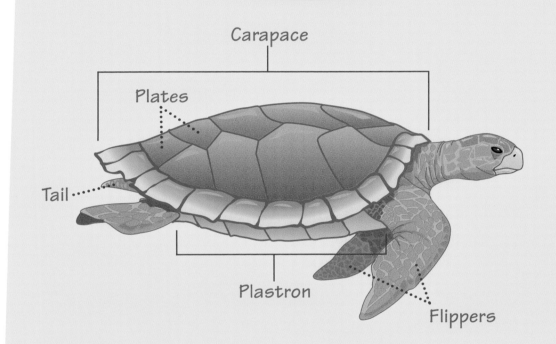

Carapace

Plates

Tail

Plastron

Flippers

Do Sea Turtles Have Teeth?

Sea turtles, like all turtles, are toothless. But they do have ridges, or bumps, along both their upper and lower jaws. These ridges are pointy and sharp. They help a turtle cut its food into small pieces before swallowing.

Most sea turtles feed on small sea animals, such as sponges. They also feed on sea plants and grasses. But some sea turtles eat mostly plants, and some eat mostly meat.

A sea turtle that feeds mostly on plants has jaws that look like the edge of a saw, as this green turtle does. This helps the turtle tear off pieces of tough plants. Meat-eating sea turtles have ridges that are as sharp as knives. With their jaws, they can slice into their prey.

Besides being sharp, the jaws of turtles are strong. Meat-eating sea turtles often use their jaws to grab passing fish. Once these turtles clamp down tightly, their prey can't slip away.

Green turtle's jaws

How Sharp Are a Sea Turtle's Senses?

A sea turtle's senses are very sharp. This reptile's sense of smell is its strongest sense. Some scientists believe that a sea turtle has a stronger sense of smell than a dog has. A sea turtle uses its keen nose to find prey and to smell a nearby enemy.

A sea turtle can hear well, too. But where are the ears of this green turtle? Sea turtles have eardrums that are covered by skin. With these eardrums, sea turtles can hear low-pitched sounds about as well as a person can hear them. The eardrums also help sea turtles detect vibrations along the ground or in the water.

Sea turtles also have good eyesight. They can see clearly when they are swimming through the water. Their eyes help them spot small prey in the open seas.

Green turtle

Are Sea Turtles Slow?

On land, sea turtles are very slow. But, in the water, they're fast. Green turtles, like the one you see here, can zip through the water at nearly 20 miles (32 kilometers) per hour.

Sea turtles have powerful front legs. These legs are long. They are also wide and flat at the end—just like paddles. Sea turtles use their strong front legs as paddles to glide swiftly through the water.

The sea turtle's shell helps it swim fast, too. Its shell is flatter and smaller than most other turtle shells. It's the perfect shape to cut through the water with the least amount of effort.

A sea turtle's small shell does have a drawback, though. Unlike many other turtles, a sea turtle can't pull its head and legs inside its shell to hide from its enemies. Instead, a sea turtle must depend on speedy swimming to get away.

Green turtle swimming

Why Do Sea Turtles Migrate?

Since sea turtles are cold-blooded, they need to stay in warm waters all year long. So when the temperature starts to drop, they migrate, or travel long distances, to warmer waters. Some sea turtles have to travel hundreds, or even thousands, of miles just to keep warm.

Sea turtles, including loggerheads, migrate for another reason, too. Female sea turtles leave the waters where they feed to travel to a nesting ground. This is where they will eventually lay their eggs. Once the females lay their eggs, they journey back to their feeding grounds.

The open sea doesn't have any landmarks. So how do migrating sea turtles know where to go? Some scientists think that sea turtles may use the sun, the moon, and the stars to guide them.

Loggerhead turtle

Where Do Sea Turtles Lay Their Eggs?

All turtles—whether they live on land, in fresh water, or in the sea—lay their eggs on land. Sea turtles lay their eggs on sandy beaches.

Many female sea turtles have what is called a homing instinct. This means that they return to the beach where they were born to lay their eggs.

Laying eggs on land is hard work for a female sea turtle. When swimming, a female can glide through the water with ease. But on a beach, she must slowly drag herself across the sand.

A female sea turtle looks for a spot that will be safe at high tide. Once she finds a safe spot, she digs a hole in the sand with her back feet. The female then lays her eggs inside the hole and covers them with sand. When she is finished, she heads toward the water and back out to sea.

Sea turtles on a beach

What Is a Sea Turtle Clutch?

A nest of turtle eggs is called a clutch. A female sea turtle may lay over 100 eggs in just one clutch! And she may lay six or more clutches in a season. Altogether, this may add up to 1,000 eggs! But most sea turtles lay far fewer eggs than that. The average is about 400 eggs in a season.

A sea turtle's egg is usually about the size and shape of a Ping-Pong ball. Its shell is not brittle like a bird's egg. Instead, it's tough and springy. It needs to be, especially if it's at the bottom of a 100-egg pile!

Over time, the sand incubates *(IHN kyuh bayts)*, or warms, the eggs. This helps the baby turtles grow inside the safety of their shells until they are ready to hatch. Most sea turtles hatch after about two months of incubation.

Sea turtle clutch

What Is Life Like for a Hatchling?

A clutch of hatchlings, or baby sea turtles, all dig their way out of their nest at the same time. Each tiny hatchling weighs about as much as a pencil and can fit in the palm of your hand.

The newborn turtles leave their nest at night. Without parents to protect them, the hatchlings must fend for themselves. Even in the darkness, many animals, such as sea gulls and crabs, prey on hatchlings. So the baby turtles must scurry across the open beach and into the water—fast!

When baby turtles reach the water, they have a long trip ahead. They must swim far out to the safer waters of the open sea. There they remain until they are young adults. Then most sea turtles return to shallow waters along the coast, where they live for most of their lives.

Sea turtle hatchling

How Long Do Sea Turtles Live?

The most dangerous part of a sea turtle's life is its first 10 years. During those years, the turtle is small and not very fast. If it survives this period, it can live a long life. Some kinds of sea turtles can live to be 80 years old. Other turtles can live even longer than that. In fact, some turtles live longer than many other creatures with backbones—including humans.

As a species, turtles have been around a long time. In fact, they are some of the world's most ancient creatures. They were probably around while dinosaurs still walked the earth.

Adult green turtle

How Did the Hawksbill Get Its Name?

The hawksbill is a colorful sea turtle that lives in warm tropical waters. This turtle has a pointed beak that looks like a hawk's bill. That's how this reptile got its name.

Unlike other sea turtles, the hawksbill has two claws on each flipper. It often uses its claws to stir up sponges that live along the ocean floor or in coral reefs. Hawksbills feed on sponges whenever they get a chance. In fact, hawksbills like sponges so much that they rarely eat anything else.

Hawksbill turtle

Which Sea Turtle Has a Soft Side?

The leatherback is the only species of turtle that lives in the sea and does not have a hard, bony shell. Its shell is covered instead with a soft, leathery skin.

The leatherback is also the largest of all turtles. This sea giant can be 8 feet (2.4 meters) long. The span of its front flippers is even longer than that. And it can weigh more than 1,500 pounds (680 kilograms). That's as much as some whales!

Most sea turtles stay in warm coastal waters. Leatherbacks, however, often go into deep northern waters off Canada and Europe and into the cool southern waters off Argentina. That's where they can find plenty of their favorite food—jellyfish.

Leatherback turtle

Are Tortoises Turtles, Too?

Turtles are an order, or large group, of reptiles. This order is divided into smaller groups called families. One of these families of turtles is the tortoise family. So, yes, tortoises are turtles, too.

Unlike sea turtles, tortoises live only on land. Like the leopard tortoise you see here, tortoises have big, heavy shells that are shaped like domes. And unlike sea turtles, they can hide inside their shells for protection. When they're frightened, tortoises just tuck their heads and tails inside their shells. Some tortoises also tuck their feet in. Other tortoises pull their front feet over their heads.

Tortoises move very slowly on land. They are the slowest of all turtles. In fact, they are the slowest of all reptiles. But in spite of being slow, the stout, short legs and feet of the tortoise are just right for walking on dry grass and rough ground.

Leopard tortoise

How Big Do Tortoises Get?

Tortoises can get very big—especially giant tortoises like the Galapagos *(guh LAH puh GOHS)* tortoise! The Galapagos is one of the largest members of the tortoise family. Some adults weigh more than 600 pounds (270 kilograms). That's as much as three or four grown men!

The Galapagos has a high, domed shell. It also has four stumpy legs that look a bit like an elephant's legs. When this tortoise walks, its enormous body rocks from side to side.

Galapagos tortoises and other giant tortoises live longer than any other land animal. It is not unusual for them to live for over one hundred years. In fact, an Aldabra tortoise from the African island nation of Seychelles *(say SHEHL)* lived 152 years!

Galapagos tortoises can be found in only one spot in the world—on the Galapagos Islands. The nearest continent, South America, is more than 600 miles (965 kilometers) away to the east!

Galapagos tortoise

How Do Galapagos Tortoises Win Over Mates?

Sometimes Galapagos males compete for the same female. One way males do this is by threatening each other with loud grunts and open jaws. This can often be enough to scare off a rival. But sometimes the only way to win over a mate is to fight.

When two males are ready to fight, they pull their heads and long necks into their shells. Then they ram into each other as hard as they can. Bang! Again and again, they slam into each other with great force.

Mating season for the Galapagos tortoises can be a noisy time. Males grunt loudly when they try to attract females. Some grunts are so loud that they can be heard almost a mile away!

Galapagos males

Do Tortoises Migrate?

Tortoises are so slow that they can't migrate to warmer habitats, as sea turtles can. But some tortoises live in places where winters can get very cold. So what do the tortoises in these places do when it gets cold? They dig burrows, which are underground shelters.

Inside their safe burrows, the tortoises hibernate, or sleep through the cold months. During this time, a tortoise's heartbeat slows. The tortoise hardly breathes at all.

When a tortoise digs a burrow for winter, it needs to dig down deep to escape the cold. Some tortoises may dig winter burrows that are up to 10 to 30 feet (3 to 9.1 meters) long! Tortoises dig with their front legs. Their broad nails and strong front limbs make the digging go quickly.

Tortoise in a burrow

Which Tortoise Is Not Afraid of the Heat?

Desert tortoises live where it's hot and dry. Some live in deserts where the temperatures can often climb above 100° Fahrenheit (38° Celsius)! But the desert tortoise knows just what to do when the temperature really rises. It burrows underground to escape the hot sun. On very hot days, this tortoise comes out only once in the early morning and once again in the late afternoon.

Since it doesn't rain often in the desert, this turtle has to make the most of it when it does rain. To "catch" the rain, the desert tortoise digs basins, or bowl-shaped holes, in the ground. At the first sign of rain, the tortoise checks back on each basin. If all goes well, the turtle gets a much-needed drink!

When the desert tortoise does find water, it drinks quite a bit. It is thirsty, but it is also storing water in its bladder. During the desert's long dry spells, the turtle's body can use this supply until it rains again.

Desert tortoise

Which Tortoise Can Flatten Itself Like a Pancake?

It's the pancake tortoise! This tortoise lives on the rocky mountains of eastern Africa. When alarmed, it scurries to a narrow crack in the cliffs. Then it squeezes snugly into the small opening.

How can the pancake tortoise do this? Unlike other tortoises, it has a very flat and soft shell. Some scientists believe that this turtle can let air out of its lungs and become even flatter. Once inside a narrow crack, the pancake tortoise fills its lungs with air and expands its shell to stay put. This turtle can fit so tightly inside the smallest of openings that most predators can't pull it out.

The pancake tortoise is an excellent climber. It can sometimes be found as high as 6,000 feet (1,829 meters) aboveground. Up there, it feeds on fresh and dried mountain grasses, as well as on wildflowers.

Pancake tortoise

What Is the Biggest Turtle Family?

Pond and marsh turtles make up the biggest family of turtles. There are just over 90 different species of them. Most live in lakes, ponds, and rivers. A few spend most of their time on land.

When swimming underwater, pond and marsh turtles need to come to the surface to breathe. Like all turtles, these turtles have lungs and need to breathe air. But turtles don't need to breathe as often as humans do. Some pond and marsh turtles take only one breath an hour!

Like sea turtles, pond and marsh turtles are good swimmers. But most pond and marsh turtles have webbed feet, while most sea turtles have feet that look like flippers. And most freshwater turtles have large hind legs and smaller front limbs. Pond and marsh turtles are much smaller than sea turtles, too. Most, like the map turtle you see here, are no bigger around than a dinner plate.

Map turtle

How Do Box Turtles "Box" Themselves In?

Box turtles are small pond and marsh turtles that live in North America. They're called box turtles with good reason. If an enemy such as a rat comes near one of these turtles, it can "box" itself up inside its shell. That's some trick!

No other turtles have shells quite like these land-dwellers. A box turtle's plastron is hinged. This lets the turtle bring the plastron right up against the carapace. Once the box turtle tucks itself in, it can close its shell up tight.

A box turtle lives most of its long life in one area of land. That area is called its home range. A box turtle's home range is usually not much bigger than two American football fields. There, the turtle can find everything it needs, such as water and soft soil for nesting. A home range also has plenty of worms, insects, and berries for the turtle to eat.

Box turtle

What Is a Terrapin?

Terrapin *(TEHR uh pihn)* is the name given to a group of turtles that live in creeks and shallow marshes along the seacoast. Water is not a terrapin's only home, though. Many terrapins live both on land and in the water. No other turtles live in such a wide variety of habitats.

In the morning, large groups of terrapins often sun themselves on the banks of a pond or a river. They stretch out their legs and heads as far as possible to soak in the sun's rays. They're not trying to get a tan, though. They're just warming themselves up after a cool dip in the water.

Diamondback terrapins live along the eastern and southern coasts of the United States. These small turtles belong to the pond and marsh turtle family. They mostly eat snails, crawfish, and water plants.

Diamondback terrapins

Which Turtles Relax on River Bottoms?

When soft-shelled turtles relax, they usually do it on muddy river bottoms. The mud is a soft place to settle down. It also hides the turtles from predators.

Once a softshell finds a good spot to rest, it can stay underwater for a very long time. Softshells do not have hard, bony shells as most other turtles do. Instead they have a round shell that is covered with thick, leathery skin. This skin lets oxygen enter the turtle's body from the surrounding water. And that lets a softshell relax a bit longer!

Softshells also have long, tube-shaped noses. They use their noses to turn over stones as they look for food, such as worms and crayfish. Softshells can also use their snouts as snorkels. When they come to the surface to breathe, just the tips of their noses peek above the water.

Soft-shelled turtle

How Did the Snapping Turtle Get Its Name?

This odd-looking turtle has a shell that looks too small for its body. It can't hide inside its shell for protection. Instead, it depends on its strong, snapping jaws for defense. When a fish swims by, the turtle stretches out its long neck, and—snap! The snapper takes its prey in the blink of an eye.

The common snapping turtle has a large head with powerful jaws. It also has a long saw-toothed tail. The snapping turtle is one of the biggest freshwater turtles. The shells of common snappers can be 19 inches (47 centimeters) long. The males grow larger than the females.

These turtles eat snails, mussels, fish, and water plants. After catching their prey, they use their hooked jaws to tear the food into bite-sized chunks.

Common snapping turtle

How Does an Alligator Snapping Turtle Fish?

The alligator snapping turtle carries its own "fishing bait" inside its mouth. In the middle of its tongue is a long, thin piece of pink flesh. When the turtle holds its mouth open, this flesh looks like a squirming worm! A hungry fish sees it, swims up close to look, and snap! The turtle has a meal.

Alligator snappers are the largest turtles in North America. Some grow more than 2 feet (60 centimeters) long and weigh over 200 pounds (91 kilograms). These turtles have hooked jaws and long, alligatorlike tails. They also have prickly scales on their necks.

Alligator snapping
turtle

What Is Odd About Side-Necked Turtles?

Most turtles are able to pull their heads directly into their shells. Side-necked turtles can't do this. Instead, they fold their heads to the side and tuck them under their shells.

There are two families of side-necked turtles. These families are snake-necked turtles and side-necked turtles. All members of these two families live in Africa, Australia, and South America.

The Australian snake-necked turtle lives in northern Australia and a few nearby islands. It grows to about 1 foot (30 centimeters) long. When frightened, this turtle releases a smelly, reddish-orange liquid from under its front legs. That's enough to discourage most predators!

Australian snake-
necked turtle

Which Turtle Is a Stinkpot?

The common musk turtle is one turtle you wouldn't want to anger. Like a skunk, this turtle releases a foul smell when it's disturbed. That's why it's often called a stinkpot.

This turtle is a member of the mud and musk turtle family. Like many members of this family, the stinkpot spends much of its time in the water. There it feeds on plants, mollusks, small fish, and insects. The stinkpot also eats carrion, which is the remains of dead animals. When looking for food, this musk turtle often walks along the bottoms of streams or ponds instead of swimming.

Stinkpots are small turtles. Few adults grow more than 6 inches (15 centimeters) long. These turtles may be tiny. But they have large heads, strong jaws, and very mean bites!

Common musk turtle

Are Turtles in Danger?

More than 40 kinds of turtles are in danger, including many types of sea turtles.

Some turtles are close to becoming extinct, or being killed off, because they are hunted for their meat and eggs. Others, like the hawksbill, are hunted for their beautiful shells, which can be made into jewelry or sold as ornaments.

Some turtles have lost their habitat, too. Their natural homes have been destroyed to make way for cities and farms. Pollution from cars and factories has poisoned the land and waters where they live as well.

Many people are working hard to protect turtles. Preserves have been set up where the turtles can live safely. Scientists also raise some endangered species on farms to keep the species alive. Further efforts like these are needed to make sure that these ancient reptiles will continue to be here for a long time to come.

Hawksbill turtle

Shelled Reptile Fun Facts

→ Some members of the mud and musk family of turtles climb trees.

→ A "turtle cleaning station" is a place where sea turtles gather to get their shells cleaned by algae-eating fish.

→ The longest turtle burrow ever found was over 46 feet (14 meters) long.

→ Some turtles can live an entire year without eating.

→ Once a male sea turtle enters the ocean, it will almost never come back on land.

→ A soft-shelled turtle can outrun a human over a short distance.

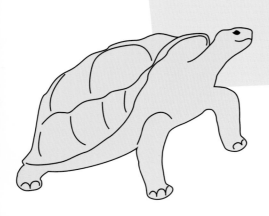
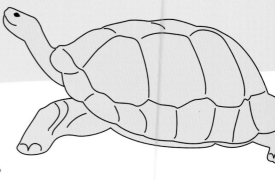

Glossary

burrow A hole dug in the ground by an animal for shelter.

carapace The shell on the back of a turtle.

carrion The remains of a dead animal.

clutch A nest of turtle eggs.

cold-blooded Having blood that is about the same temperature as the air or water around the animal.

eardrum A thin, flat part of an ear that vibrates when sound waves strike it.

extinct No longer existing.

flipper A broad, flat limb used for swimming.

habitat The place where an animal lives.

hatchling A baby turtle.

hibernate To spend a long period in deep sleep.

home range An area of land or water where an animal spends much of its life.

homing instinct A natural feeling to return to a certain area.

incubate To warm eggs in order to hatch them.

migrate To move from one place to settle in another.

mollusk An animal with no backbone and a soft body that is often covered by a shell.

musk A substance with a strong and lasting odor.

nesting ground A place used by an animal to build its nest.

plastron The shell on the under part of a turtle.

predator An animal that preys upon another.

prey An animal that is hunted for food by another animal.

reptile A cold-blooded animal with a backbone that uses lungs to breathe.

sponge An animal that lives in water where it attaches itself to stones or plants.

Index

(**Boldface** indicates a photo or illustration.)

For more information about sea turtles, try these resources:

Interrupted Journey: Saving Endangered Sea Turtles, by Kathryn Lasky, Candlewick Press, 2001

Animals of the Ocean: Sea Turtles, by Sally Dunbier, David Bateman Ltd., 2000

Sea Turtles, by Gail Gibbons, Holiday House, 1998

http://octopus.gma.org/turtles/index.html
http://www.turtles.org/
http://www.nwf.org/wildthornberrys/seaturtle.html

Turtle Classification

Scientists classify animals by placing them into groups. The animal kingdom is a group that contains all the world's animals. Phylum, class, order, and family are smaller groups. Each phylum contains many classes. A class contains orders, an order contains families, and a family contains individual species. Each species also has its own scientific name. Here is how the animals in this book fit in to this system.

Animals with backbones and their relatives (Phylum Chordata)

Reptiles (Class Reptilia)

Turtles (Order Testudines)

Leatherback sea turtle (Family Dermochelyidae)

Leatherback . . . . *Dermochelys coriacea*

Pond, Marsh, etc. (Family Emydidae)

Common map turtle . . . . *Graptemys geographica*
Diamondback terrapin . . . . *Malaclemys terrapin*

Sea turtle (Family Cheloniidae)

Green turtle . . . . *Chelonia mydas*
Hawksbill . . . . *Eretmochelys imbricata*
Kemp's ridley . . . . *Lepidochelys kempii*
Loggerhead . . . . *Caretta caretta*
Olive ridley . . . . *Lepidochelys olivacea*

Soft-shelled turtles (Family Trionychidae)

Tortoises (Family Testudinidae)

Desert tortoise . . . . *Gopherus agassizii*
Gopher tortoise . . . . *Gopherus polyphemus*